Knowing God's Will made easier

Mark Water

HENDRICKSON PUBLISHERS

Knowing God's Will Made Easier
Hendrickson Publishers, Inc.
P.O. Box 3473
Peabody, Massachusetts 01961-3473

Copyright © 1998 John Hunt
Publishing
Text copyright © 1998 Mark Water

ISBN 1-56563-376-8

Original edition published in English
under the title *Knowing God's Will
Made Easier* by John Hunt
Publishing, Alresford, Hants, UK.

Designed and produced
by Tony Cantale Graphics

First printing April 1998
Reprinted April 1999, 2001, 2002

Printed in Hong Kong / China

Unless otherwise noted, Scripture
quotations are taken from HOLY
BIBLE, NEW INTERNATIONAL
VERSION copyright © 1973, 1978,
1984 by International Bible
Society. All rights reserved.

Quotations on p.36 from
Lamentations and 1 Peter taken
from *Revised Standard Version*,
copyright © Thomas Nelson &
Sons 1946 & 1952.

Photography supplied by Foxx
Photos, Goodshoot, Digital Vision
and Tony Cantale

Illustrations by
Tony Cantale Graphics

Contents

Special pull-out chart
A bird's-eye view of God's guidance in the Bible

There's no secret formula to discover

No special button to press

Finding out about God's will is not like logging on to the Internet and pressing an icon labeled "Knowing God's Will," which will then display everything you want to know.

In the Bible, God has given us a number of general principles for guidance. We are expected to know what these are and to follow them. There are dozens of such principles. Here are just two of them.

Ask

Do you lack wisdom? Here is God's remedy to that: "Ask!"

"If any of you lacks wisdom, he should ask God, who gives generously to all without finding fault, and it will be given to him." *James 1:5*

Ask as if you mean it!

Jesus stressed that people should be in earnest when they prayed: "So I say to you: ask and it will be given to you; seek and you will find; knock and the door will be opened to you. For everyone who asks receives; he who seeks finds; and to him who knocks, the door will be opened." *Luke 11:9-10*

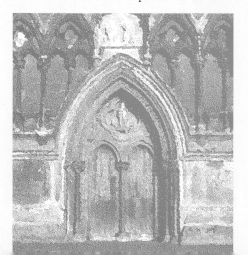

Why shouldn't we ask for signs – Gideon did?

Gideon puts God to the test

"Gideon said to God, 'If you will save Israel by my hand as you have promised – look, I will place a wool fleece on the threshing-floor. If there is dew only on the fleece and all the ground is dry, then I will know that you will save Israel by my hand, as you said.' And this is what happened. Gideon rose early the next day; he squeezed the fleece and wrung out the dew – a bowlful of water.

Then Gideon said to God, 'Do not be angry with me. Let me make just one more request. Allow me one more test with the fleece. This time make the fleece dry and the ground covered with dew.' That night God did so. Only the fleece was dry; all the ground was covered with dew." *Judges 6:36-40*

What is the Bible telling us?

When you read Bible stories, ask yourself whether they are giving a warning to heed, or an example to follow.

The Bible tells us about both the good and the bad sides of Gideon's character.

Gideon's good points	Gideon's bad points
• He was humble. "I am the least in my family." *Judges 6:15* • He obeyed God. "Gideon ... did as the LORD told him." *Judges 6:27* • He experienced God's Spirit. "The Spirit of the LORD came upon Gideon." *Judges 6:34* • He was a clever strategist. *Judges 7:16-18* • He was diplomatic. *Judges 8:1-3*	• Gideon was not content with the first miracle, a wet fleece on a dry background. He had to ask for a second (and more difficult) miracle, a dry fleece on a wet background. • It looks as if Gideon himself knew that what he was doing was wrong. He said, "Do not be angry with me."

Gideon showed great courage and served God faithfully in many ways. But this does not mean to say he never did anything wrong. His whole story is told in Judges 6–8.

Jesus condemns people seeking a sign

When Jesus went preaching and healing, instead of believing in him, some people asked for a sign that he was the Son of God. Jesus said, "This is a wicked generation. It asks for a miraculous sign, but none will be given it except the sign of Jonah."
Luke 11:29

How does the Bible say God guides us?

The Old Testament

The Old Testament gives many examples of people who were guided by God in a variety of ways.

Person	Incident	Bible reference
Abraham	God sends Abraham to Canaan	*Genesis 12*
Abraham's servant	The servant looks for a suitable wife for Isaac	*Genesis 24*
Jacob	God shows Jacob how to take the best goats from Laban	*Genesis 31*
God's people	God provides a pillar of fire to guide the people in the desert	*Exodus 13:21*
Joshua	God guides Joshua through sacred lots	*Joshua 18:10*
God's people	God provides prophets to tell the people his will	*Deuteronomy 18:14-19*
Saul	Saul uses lots to discover who has broken the fast	*1 Samuel 14:41-43*

The New Testament

People in the New Testament were guided by God in "supernatural" ways.

Person	Incident	Bible reference
Joseph	God tells Joseph, in a dream, to escape to Egypt	*Matthew 2:13-15*
Philip	An angel tells Philip to go to the desert road	*Acts 8:26-40*
Cornelius	God speaks to Cornelius in a vision	*Acts 10:1-8*
Peter	God speaks to Peter through a trance, as he prays	*Acts 10:9-23*
Pilate's wife	God warns Pilate's wife through a disturbing dream	*Matthew 27:19*
Church leaders	The Holy Spirit guides the Council at Jerusalem	*Acts 15:1-29*

An angel directs Philip to the treasurer of Candace

"Now an angel of the Lord said to Philip, 'Go south to the road – the desert road – that goes down from Jerusalem to Gaza.' So he started out, and on his way he met an Ethiopian eunuch, an important official in charge of all the treasury of Candace, Queen of the Ethiopians. ... Philip ... told him the good news about Jesus ... and baptized him. When they came up out of the water, the Spirit of the Lord suddenly took Philip away, and the eunuch did not see him again, but went on his way rejoicing."
Acts 8:26-27, 35, 38-39

What can stop me from knowing God's will?

Warnings in the Old Testament

• Deliberate sin
"If I cherished sin in my heart,
   the Lord would not have
   listened;
but God has surely listened
   and heard my voice in prayer."
Psalm 66:18-19

• Turning a deaf ear to people in need
"If a man shuts his ears to the cry
   of the poor,
   he too will cry out and not be
   answered."
Proverbs 21:13

• Ignoring God's teaching
"If anyone turns a deaf ear to the
   law,
even his prayers are detestable."
Proverbs 28:9

• Active participation in evil
"The eyes of the LORD are on the
   righteous
   and his ears are attentive to their
   cry;
the face of the LORD is against
   those who do evil,
   to cut off the memory of them
   from the earth."
Psalm 34:15-16

James

James points out four things to avoid if we want to know God's will and serve him in the right way.

• Failing to ask God
"You do not have, because you do not ask God." *James 4:2*

• Asking in the wrong way
"You do not receive, because you ask with wrong motives, that you may spend what you get on your pleasures." *James 4:2-3*

• Having doubts that God gives generously
"But when he asks, he must believe and not doubt, because he who doubts is like a wave of the sea, blown and tossed by the wind. That man should not think he will receive anything from the Lord." *James 1:6-7*

• Asking in a proud way
"God opposes the proud but gives grace to the humble." *James 4:6; quoting Proverbs 3:34*

Jesus teaches about prayer

• Have a forgiving spirit
Jesus taught that in order to receive forgiveness, we must forgive. This principle also applies to prayer and to seeking God's will. "For if you forgive men when they sin against you, your heavenly Father will also forgive you. But if you do not forgive men their sins, your Father will not forgive your sins."
Matthew 6:14-15

• Make it up with people before you pray to God
"Therefore, if you are offering your gift at the altar and there remember that your brother has something against you, leave your gift there in front of the altar. First go and be reconciled to your brother; then come and offer your gift." *Matthew 5:23-24*

Trusting God does not mean we don't need friends!

Iron sharpens iron
"As iron sharpens iron, so one man sharpens another."
Proverbs 27:17

The apostle Paul is comforted
It is instructive to see how the "super-spiritual" apostle Paul was once comforted by God. Was it through a vision? Was it through prayer? Was it through a miraculous event? Or did God comfort Paul through a worship service?

No doubt God did "speak" to Paul in these ways, but Paul was also comforted by a Christian friend. He was anxiously waiting for news about the Christians at Corinth. Paul writes, "God, who comforts the downcast, comforted us by the coming of Titus." *2 Corinthians 7:6*

For Paul, there was no conflict in trusting God and being comforted by a friend.

Characteristics of a good friend
The Book of Proverbs advises us to choose our friends carefully.

"A righteous man is cautious in friendship."
Proverbs 12:26

"He who walks with the wise grows wise,
    but a companion of fools suffers harm."
Proverbs 13:20

It may be that you can be a friend to someone who is seeking God's guidance for his or her life.

Friends found in the Book of Proverbs
• Loyal friends   *Proverbs 17:17; 27:10*
• Trusted friends   *Proverbs 27:6*
• A special friend   *Proverbs 18:24*

Jesus is a friend

• "You are my friends if you do what I command." *John 15:14*
• "I no longer call you servants. ... Instead, I have called you friends." *John 15:15*

God as a friend

• "The LORD would speak to Moses face to face, as a man speaks with his friend." *Exodus 33:11*

See also: *Key 7: Ask a friend,* page 28

Nine keys to finding God's will

Nine keys
Pages 16-33 give nine keys to finding God's will.

Checklist

☐	Key 1: Be humble.	☐
☐	Key 2: Pray.	☐
☐	Key 3: Follow the light you already have.	☐
☐	Key 4: Don't give up.	☐
☐	Key 5: Don't be put off by barriers.	☐
☐	Key 6: Use your mind.	☐
☐	Key 7: Ask a friend.	☐
☐	Key 8: Remember, God is not in a hurry.	☐
☐	Key 9: Trust God.	☐

Look at the instructions for each key. How good are you at following each instruction? Try putting them into order, with your best at the top, and so on. For example, if you are good at using your mind, put it high on your list. If you are not so good at asking friends for advice, put that key low on your list.

Use the left-hand column of boxes for your list. Use the righthand column of boxes for a checkmark when you have read the appropriate pages.

Now start with the bottom item on your list, and turn to the relevant page.

Guidance is a relationship
Guidance is not a puzzle to be solved, but a relationship with Jesus. The closer we are to Jesus, the less anxious we will be about knowing God's will for our lives.

• "I am the true vine"
What relationship could be closer than the way a vine branch is linked to the main stem of the vine? Jesus said, "I am the true vine. ...Remain in me, and I will remain in you. ...I am the vine;

you are the branches. If a man remains in me and I in him, he will bear much fruit; apart from me you can do nothing."
John 15:1, 4-5

• A promise to hang on to
"God has said, 'Never will I leave you; never will I forsake you.'"
Hebrews 13:5

Key 1: Be humble

A proud person

A proud person may miss out on God's guidance simply through not being prepared to pray to God about it.

A characteristic of humility is to be contrite or repentant: "This is the one I esteem: he who is humble and contrite in spirit, and trembles at my word." *Isaiah 66:2*

Humility linked with ...

Seeking God	"Seek the Lord, all you humble."	*Zephaniah 2:3*
The meek	"I will leave within you the meek and humble, who trust in the name of the Lord."	*Zephaniah 3:12*
Gentleness	Jesus said, "I am gentle and humble in heart."	*Matthew 11:29*
Gentleness	"Be completely humble and gentle."	*Ephesians 4:2*
Other people	"In humility consider others better than yourselves."	*Philippians 2:3*

Blessings received by the humble

"The Lord *sustains* the humble."	*Psalm 147:6*
"[The Lord] *gives grace* to the humble."	*Proverbs 3:34*
"God opposes the proud but *gives grace* to the humble."	*1 Peter 5:5*
"Whoever humbles himself will be *exalted*."	*Matthew 23:12*
"I live in a high and holy place, but also with him who is contrite and lowly in spirit, *to revive the spirit* of the lowly and *to revive the heart* of the contrite."	*Isaiah 57:15*

The supreme example of humility – "he humbled himself"

"Your attitude should be the same as that of Christ Jesus:
Who, being in very nature God,
  did not consider equality with God something to be grasped,
but made himself nothing,
  taking the very nature of a servant,
  being made in human likeness.
And being found in appearance as a man,
  he humbled himself
  and became obedient to death – even death on a cross!"
Philippians 2:5-8

Concluding thought

"All of you, clothe yourselves with humility towards one
  another." *1 Peter 5:5*

Key 2: Pray

Dependence on God
Prayer shows dependence on God.

Who prayed in the Old Testament?

Person	Prayer	Bible reference
Abraham	For the city of Sodom	*Genesis 18:22-33*
Abraham's servant	For guidance	*Genesis 24:12-14*
Moses	A song of thanksgiving	*Exodus 15*
Hannah	For a son	*1 Samuel 1*
David	A song of thanksgiving	*2 Samuel 22*
Solomon	For wisdom	*1 Kings 3*
Nehemiah	For his nation	*Nehemiah 1*
Nebuchadnezzar	Praising God	*Daniel 4*
Jonah	A cry for help	*Jonah 2*
Habakkuk	For mercy	*Habakkuk 3*

Jesus in Gethsemane

"[Jesus] withdrew about a stone's throw beyond [his disciples], knelt down and prayed, *'Father, if you are willing, take this cup from me; yet not my will, but yours be done.'* An angel from heaven appeared to him and strengthened him. And being in anguish, he prayed more earnestly, and his sweat was like drops of blood falling to the ground." *Luke 22:41-44*

What position should we be in when we pray?

The Bible does not give any rules about whether we should sit, stand, or kneel to pray.

Kneeling

• **Jesus sometimes knelt to pray.**
In the Garden of Gethsemane Jesus "knelt down and prayed" (*Luke 22:41*) and this may have given rise to the Christian custom of kneeling in prayer.

• **At times, Paul knelt to pray.**
"For this reason I kneel before the Father." *Ephesians 3:14*

• **Some of Paul's Christian friends knelt to pray.**
"When [Paul] had said this, he knelt down with all of them and prayed." *Acts 20:36*
"All the disciples and their wives and children accompanied us out of the city, and there on the beach we knelt to pray." *Acts 21:5*

• **Daniel prayed three times a day on his knees.**
"Now when Daniel learned that the decree had been published, he went home to his upstairs room where the windows opened towards Jerusalem. Three times a day he got down on his knees and prayed, giving thanks to God, just has he had done before."
Daniel 6:10
Daniel ended up being thrown to the lions because of this open worship of God.

Hands lifted up

"I want men everywhere to lift up holy hands in prayer, without anger or disputing." *1 Timothy 2:8*

Standing up

Jews stand up to pray. Solomon stood as he prayed. He also lifted up his hands as a indication that he was praying.
"Then Solomon stood before the altar of the LORD in front of the whole assembly of Israel, spread out his hands toward heaven and [prayed]."
1 Kings 8:21

Hearts not bodies

The position of our bodies in prayer is not half so important as the attitude of our hearts. For "the LORD weighs the heart." *Proverbs 21:2*

Key 3: Follow the light you already have

A lamp, not a searchlight
God does not often give Christians "long-range" guidance about their future. It is more often just about the next step to take.

The psalmist said to God, "Your word is a lamp to my feet and a light for my path." *Psalm 119:105*

God's word was a "lamp" so he could see where he was walking, not a searchlight shining on his destination.

Do you really want to know the future?
It is not always to our advantage to know what is going to happen to us. Jesus told Peter, "When you are old you will

stretch out your hands, and someone else will dress you and lead you where you do not want to go." *John 21:18*. This is probably a prediction of Peter's future martyrdom when, according to tradition, he would be killed by crucifixion.

We may be glad not to know all that will happen to us, later on in our lives.

What about other Christians?

We are not meant to pry into what God's will is for other Christians. Peter made this mistake.

"Peter turned and saw that the disciple whom Jesus loved [John] was following them. ...When Jesus saw him he asked [Jesus], 'Lord, what about him?' Jesus answered, 'If I want him to remain alive until I return, what is that to you? You must follow me.'" *John 21:20-22*

We'll never know all we want to know

• The Bible never claims to tell us about everything.
• The Bible is primarily about salvation.
• The answers to what we need to know about salvation are found it its pages.
• "When he, the Spirit of truth, comes, he will guide you into all truth." *John 16:13*

Loving and obeying

Jesus said, "If anyone loves me, he will obey my teaching." *John 14:23*

It is often easier to be preoccupied with the future than to obey Jesus in the present.

Obedience and its links	
Obedience linked with faith	*Romans 16:26*
Obedience linked with holiness	*Acts 26:18*
Obedience linked with righteousness	*Romans 6:13*
Obedience linked with God's blessing	*Deuteronomy 11:27*
Obedience linked with God's word	*Psalm 119:67*
Obedience linked with salvation	*Hebrews 5:9*

Key 4: Don't give up

Persevere

Jesus told two parables which both had the same moral to them. They were both aimed at encouraging his followers to keep praying.

Clearly, persevering in prayer is something that Christians have always found hard.

• The parable of the widow who wouldn't take "No" for an answer

"Then Jesus told his disciples a parable to show them that they should always pray and not give up. He said: 'In a certain town there was a judge who neither feared God nor cared about men. And there was a widow in that town who kept coming to him with the plea, "Grant me justice against my adversary."

'For some time he refused. But finally he said to himself, "Even though I don't fear God or care about men, yet because this widow keeps bothering me, I will see that she gets justice, so that she won't eventually wear me out with her coming!"'

And the Lord said, 'Listen to what the unjust judge says. And will not God bring about justice for his chosen ones, who cry out to him day and night? Will he keep putting them off? I tell you, he will see that they get justice, and quickly. However, when the Son of Man comes, will he find faith on the earth?'"
Luke 18:1-8

• The parable of the friend at midnight

"Then [Jesus] said to them, 'Suppose one of you has a friend, and he goes to him at midnight and says, "Friend, lend me three loaves of bread, because a friend of mine on a journey has come to me, and I have nothing to set before him."

'Then the one inside answers, "Don't bother me. The door is already locked, and my children are with me in bed. I can't get up and give you anything." I tell you, though he will not get up and give him the bread because he is his friend, yet because of the man's boldness he will get up and give him as much as he needs.'"
Luke 11:5-8

Keep on going

Perseverence is specifically needed by Christians seeking God's guidance for their lives.

Christians need to persevere in

- Running the Christian race. *Hebrews 12:1*
- Serving God. *Revelation 2:19*
- How they live and what they believe. *1 Timothy 4:16*
- Having confidence in God and doing his will. *Hebrews 10:35-36*

Key 5: Don't be put off by barriers

A pioneer missionary with a tough skin

If Paul had been deflected from carrying out God's will in his life by the avalanche of events that happened to him, we would have been deprived of our greatest missionary and theologian.

Paul's trials

Paul left a record of some of the sufferings he gladly endured for the sake of Jesus, in 1 Corinthians 4:10-13 and 2 Corinthians 11:23-28.

- He was frequently imprisoned.
- He was severely flogged.
- He was exposed to death again and again.
- He received 195 lashes from the Jews alone.
- He was beaten three times with rods.
- He was stoned.
- He was shipwrecked.
- He spent a night and a day in the open sea.
- He was constantly on the move.
- He was in danger from rivers.
- He was in danger from bandits.
- He was in danger from his own countrymen.
- He was in danger from Gentiles.
- He was in danger in the city.
- He was in danger in the country.
- He was in danger at sea.
- He was in danger from false brethren.
- He experienced hunger, thirst, cold, and sometimes went around in rags.
- He was a fool for Christ's sake.
- He was dishonored.
- He was brutally treated.
- He was made homeless.
- He was cursed.
- He was persecuted.
- He was slandered.

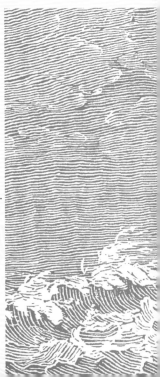

Setbacks

The setbacks we have experienced in our own lives become insignificant when compared with what some Christian missionaries and martyrs have suffered for Jesus.

Nevertheless, we all have our own problems: "For each one should carry his own load." *Galatians 6:5*

Helping others

The Bible tells us to help other people carry the loads which weigh them down and burden their lives: "Carry each other's burdens, and in this way you will fulfill the law of Christ." *Galatians 6:2*

A promise to hang on to

Jesus said, "And surely I am with you always, to the very end of the age." *Matthew 28:20*

Key 6:
Use your mind

Rational creatures
God made us with wonderful minds. We are meant to use them to the fullest – not least of all when it comes to finding out God's will for our lives.

Not like brute beasts
God promised the psalmist that his mind would be taught and informed:
"I will instruct you and teach you
  in the way you should go;
  I will counsel you and watch over
  you.
Do not be like the horse or the
  mule,
  which have no understanding
  but must be controlled by bit
  and bridle
  or they will not come to you."
Psalm 32:8-9

Paul used his mind for God
Paul, the theologian, was a great strategist. He worked out how he would set about spreading the gospel of Jesus throughout the known world. He aimed mainly at centers of population, the cities.

• He debated
"[Paul] talked and debated with the Grecian Jews, but they tried to kill him." *Acts 9:29*
• He argued persuasively
"Paul entered the synagogue and spoke boldly there for three months, arguing persuasively about the kingdom of God."
Acts 19:8
• He reasoned
"[Paul] reasoned in the synagogues with the Jews and the God-fearing Greeks, as well as in the marketplace day by day."
Acts 17:17

Apollos used his mind for God too

"[Apollos] vigorously refuted the Jews in public debate, proving from the Scriptures that Jesus was the Christ." *Acts 18:28*

"Love the Lord with your mind"

• In the Old Testament we read: "Hear, O Israel...Love the LORD your God with all your heart and with all your soul and with all your strength." *Deuteronomy 6:4-5*
• In the New Testament we read: "Jesus replied: "Love the Lord your God with all your heart and with all your soul and with all your mind."" *Matthew 22:37*
• Peter
Peter wrote: "Prepare your minds for action." *1 Peter 1:13*

Key 7: Ask a friend

David and Jonathan

One of God's greatest gifts is friendship. "Jonathan became one in spirit with David, and he loved him as himself." *1 Samuel 18:1*

Ask a friend to pray for you

Ask a friend to pray that you may know God's guidance.
It can be quite a humbling experience to share personal prayer requests with a friend. Paul often asked his trusted Christian friends to pray for him.

Paul's requests for prayer

• Boldness to preach the gospel
"Pray also for me, that whenever I open my mouth, words may be given me so that I will fearlessly make known the mystery of the gospel, for which I am an ambassador in chains. Pray that I may declare it fearlessly, as I should." *Ephesians 6:19-20*

• Physical safety
"Pray that I may be rescued from the unbelievers in Judea." *Romans 15:31*

• Opportunity to preach about Jesus
"And pray for us, too, that God may open a door for our message, so that we may proclaim the mystery of Christ, for which I am in chains." *Colossians 4:3*

• General request for prayer
"Brothers, pray for us." *1 Thessalonians 5:25*

Friends can get it wrong

Christian friends are not infallible.
Paul had to ignore the advice given to him by well-meaning Christians who urged him not to go to Jerusalem, even though their advice came "through the Spirit." *See Acts 21:4.*

Paul also prayed for his Christian friends

It seems that it was quite normal for Christians to ask for help from each other in this way in the early Church.

Paul prayed for:
• Christians at Colosse, so that they would have knowledge of God's will. *Colossians 1:9*
• Christians at Ephesus, so that they would be rooted in love. *Ephesians 3:17*
• Christians at Thessalonica, so that Jesus would be glorified in them. *2 Thessalonians 1:11-12*

A prayer for the Ephesians

"For this reason I kneel before the Father, from whom his whole family in heaven and on earth derives its name. I pray that out of his glorious riches he may strengthen you with power through his Spirit in your inner being, so that Christ may dwell in your hearts through faith. And I pray that you, being rooted and established in love, may have power, together with all the saints, to grasp how wide and long and high and deep is the love of Christ, and to know this love that surpasses knowlege – that you may be filled to the measure of all the fulness of God."
Ephesians 3:14-19

See also: *Trusting God does not mean we don't need friends!*, page 12

Key 8: Remember,
God is not in a hurry

God's timescale

God's view of time and our view of time are often very different.

We tend to be in a rush to achieve things, but God is never in a hurry.

Peter writes: "Dear friends: with the Lord a day is like a thousand years, and a thousand years are like a day." *2 Peter 3:8*

Before time

Before time, as we know it, God was active.

In creation	"In the beginning God created the heavens."	*Genesis 1:1*
In choosing us	"[God] chose us in him before the creation of the world."	*Ephesians 1:4*

A time for everything

The writer of the Book of Ecclesiastes emphasizes that everything happens at God's appointed time.

A time for ...
"There is a time for everything,
and a season for every activity under heaven:
a time to be born and a time to die,
a time to plant and a time to uproot,
a time to kill and a time to heal,
a time to tear down and a time to build,
a time to weep and a time to laugh,
a time to mourn and a time to dance,
a time to scatter stones and a time to gather them,
a time to embrace and a time to refrain,
a time to search and a time to give up,
a time to keep and a time to throw away,
a time to tear and a time to mend,
a time to be silent and a time to speak,
a time to love and a time to hate,
a time for war and a time for peace."
Ecclesiastes 3:1-8

God is your creator

"Remember your Creator in the days of your youth." *Ecclesiastes 12:1*

Key 9: Trust God

Daniel's three friends

Shadrach, Meshach and Abednego
are fine examples of people who
completely trusted God. When
they were about to be thrown
into a fiery furnace, for not
bowing down and worshipping
King Nebuchadnezzar's image of
gold, they said to the king:

"O Nebuchadnezzar, we do not
need to defend ourselves before
you in this matter. If we are thrown
into the blazing furnace, the God
we serve is able to save us from it,
and he will rescue us from your
hand, O king. But even if
he does not, we want you
to know, O king, that we
will not serve your gods
or worship the
image of gold
you have set
up." *Daniel
3:16-18*

Trusting God

When to trust God
• At all times. "Trust in him at all times, O people." *Psalm 62:8*

How to trust God
• With all your heart. "Trust in the LORD with all your heart and lean not on your own understanding." *Proverbs 3:5*
• In quietness. "In quietness and trust is your strength." *Isaiah 30:15*

Why trust God?
• Because of God's unfailing love. "But I trust in your unfailing love." *Psalm 13:5*

The result of trusting God
• Lack of fear. "I will trust and not be afraid." *Isaiah 12:2*
• God's care. "He cares for those who trust in him." *Nahum 1:7*
• Safety. "Whoever trusts in the LORD is kept safe." *Proverbs 29:25*

What should not be trusted
• Chariots (representing human power). "Some trust in chariots." *Psalm 20:7*
• Gold (representing human wealth). "If I have put my trust in gold." *Job 31:24*
• Extortion. "Do not trust in extortion." *Psalm 62:10*
• Deceptive words. "Do not trust in deceptive words." *Jeremiah 7:4*

Prayers for approaching death
The dying prayers of Jesus and Stephen express their trust in God.
• As Jesus hung dying on the cross, he prayed: "Father, into your hands I commit my spirit." *Luke 23:46*
• As Stephen was being stoned to death, he prayed: "Lord Jesus, receive my spirit." *Acts 7:59*

A promise to hang on to
"Cast all your anxiety on [God] because he cares for you."
1 Peter 5:7

Visions and dreams

The Old Testament
God's will was often revealed to people through their dreams.

People in the Old Testament who had special dreams

Jacob in Bethel	*Genesis 28:12*
Joseph	*Genesis 37:5-11*
Jacob in Haran	*Genesis 31:10-13*
A Midianite soldier	*Judges 7:13*
Solomon in Gibeon	*1 Kings 3:5*
Nebuchadnezzar	*Daniel 2*
Daniel	*Daniel 7:1*

Dreams surrounding Jesus' birth and early years
Jesus was protected in his early years through the dreams of his foster father, Joseph.

• Dream number one
"The Lord appeared to [Joseph] in a dream and said, 'Joseph son of David, do not be afraid to take Mary home as your wife, because what is conceived in her is from the Holy Spirit.'" *Matthew 1:20*

• Dream number two
"An angel of the Lord appeared to Joseph in a dream. 'Get up,' he said, 'take the child and his mother and escape to Egypt. Stay there until I tell you, for Herod is going to search for the child to kill him.'" *Matthew 2:13*

• Dream number three
"After Herod died, an angel of the Lord appeared in a dream to Joseph in Egypt and said, 'Get up, take the child and his mother and go to the land of Israel, for those who were trying to take the child's life are dead.'" *Matthew 2:19-20*

Joseph's obedience
We may feel that it was easy for Joseph. After all, he was told exactly what to do in his dreams. But he still had to do the hard part – obey God's will. "To obey is better than sacrifice."
1 Samuel 15:22

Beware

- "Much dreaming and many words are meaningless. Therefore stand in awe of God." *Ecclesiastes 5:7*
- Jeremiah wrote: "I have heard what the prophets say who prophesy lies in my name. They say, 'I had a dream! I had a dream!'" *Jeremiah 23:25*

Visions and dreams

Visions were revelations from God, which occurred while the prophet was in a dream-like state. *See Genesis 46:2; Luke 1:22.*

Visions were another important way God gave directions to people. God used dreams as a way of revealing his will, but dreams were to be tested against *written* revelation. *See Deuteronomy 13:1-5.*

God said to Miriam and Aaron,
"When a prophet of the LORD is among you,
I reveal myself to him in visions,
I speak to him in dreams."
Numbers 12:6

Paul's vision

"During the night Paul had a vision of a man of Macedonia standing and begging him, 'Come over to Macedonia and help us.' After Paul had seen the vision, we got ready at once to leave for Macedonia, concluding that God had called us to preach the gospel to them." *Acts 16:9-10*

This vision resulted in the gospel being preached in Europe for the first time.

The hardest part – waiting

Waiting "for" and waiting "on"
Waiting for guidance is often a very tough experience. This time can be used positively to wait on God:
> "The LORD is good to everyone who trusts in him,
> So it is best for us to wait in patience."
> *Lamentations 3:25 RSV*

Patience is a fruit of the Spirit
"The fruit of the Spirit is love, joy, peace, patience, kindness, goodness, faithfulness, gentleness and self-control." *Galatians 5:22-23*

Patience is one of the most necessary Christian qualities, when God's guidance seems hard to find or difficult to follow.
    Christians are told: "Be patient with everyone."
1 Thessalonians 5:14

Christians need patience for

• Facing trials
"The testing of your faith develops perseverance. Perseverance must finish its work so that you may be mature and complete, not lacking anything."
James 1:3-4

• Enduring persecution
"If when you do right and suffer for it you take it patiently, you have God's approval." *1 Peter 2:20 RSV*

• Living each day for Jesus
"Let us throw off everything that hinders and the sin that so easily entangles, and let us run with perseverance the race marked out for us." *Hebrews 12:1*

• Receiving God's promises
"You need to persevere so that when you have done the will of God, you will receive what he has promised." *Hebrews 10:36*

• Waiting for Jesus' return
"Be patient, then, brothers, until the Lord's coming." *James 5:7*

A promise to hang on to
"Blessed are all who wait for [the Lord]."
Isaiah 30:18

What to do when God seems distant

God "speaks" to Elijah

Elijah found that God "spoke" to him in a most unexpected way – in hushed tones.

Not in the wind, earthquake or fire

"The LORD said [to Elijah], 'Go and stand on the mountain in the presence of the LORD, for the LORD is about to pass by.'

Then a great and powerful wind tore the mountains apart and shattered the rocks before the LORD, but the LORD was not in the wind. After the wind there was an earthquake, but the LORD was not in the earthquake. After the earthquake came a fire, but the LORD was not in the fire. And after the fire came a gentle whisper. When Elijah heard it, he pulled his cloak over his face and went out and stood at the mouth of the cave."
1 Kings 19:11-13

Finding the meaning of God's silences

If God seems far away, it is not necessarily a sign that we have done anything wrong or that we are being punished by him. It may be because:

• God has spoken but we have paid no attention.
"But since you rejected me when I called
and no one gave heed when I stretched out my hand."
Proverbs 1:24

• He is confounding the powerful and proud.

"[Herod] plied [Jesus] with many questions, but Jesus gave him no answer." *Luke 23:9*

• He is testing our faith in Jesus.

"A Canaanite woman ... came to [Jesus], crying out, 'Lord, Son of David, have mercy on me! My daughter is suffering terribly from demon-possession.' Jesus did not answer a word." *Matthew 15:22-23*

(The next verses show how Jesus' silence drew out the woman's faith. Jesus then went on to heal her daughter.)

When God seems far away from us

In the Old Testament, many of God's followers had such an experience, and through it came closer to God.

The psalmist pleads with God, "Do not hide your face from me." This possibility made him redouble his efforts to seek God. "My heart says of you, 'Seek his face!' Your face, Lord, I will seek." *Psalm 27:8-9*

What to do
when you let God down

When things go wrong
If things go wrong, it is easy to allow a situation to go from bad to worse. When we've let God down once, it becomes easy to do it again and again, if we are not careful.

Forbidden
The Bible makes it quite clear that we should never seek God's will through any occult practices.

"When you enter the land the LORD your God is giving you, do not learn to imitate the detestable ways of the nations there. Let no one be found among you who sacrifices his son or daughter in the fire, who practices divination or sorcery, interprets omens, engages in witchcraft, or casts spells, or who is a medium or spiritist or who consults the dead. Anyone who does these things is detestable to the LORD, and because of these detestable practices the LORD your God will drive out those nations before you.

You must be blameless before the Lord your God."
Deuteronomy 18:9-13

Saul and David compared

Saul
When things went particularly poorly for Saul, he turned to a medium.

• Saul's mistake
"Saul then said to his attendants, "Find me a woman who is a medium, so that I may go and inquire of her." " *1 Samuel 28:7 (The whole story is in 1 Samuel 28:6-25)*

• Saul's epitaph
"Saul died because he was unfaithful to the LORD; he did not keep the word of the LORD, and even consulted a medium for guidance, and did not inquire of the LORD. So the LORD put him to death and turned the kingdom over to David son of Jesse." *1 Chronicles 10:13-14*

Footnote David is remembered as God's most faithful king of Israel. "The LORD has sought out a man after his own heart." *1 Samuel 13:14.* David became such a person.

David

David, in severe difficulties, turned back to God.

• David's sins

David had committed adultery with Bathsheba. He then arranged for Bathsheba's husband, Uriah, to be killed in battle. See 2 Samuel 11–12. What could an adulterer and murderer do about this situation?

• David's return

We have a record of what David did. He confessed his sin to God.

"Have mercy on me, O God,
  according to your unfailing love;
according to your great compassion
  blot out my transgressions.
Wash away all my iniquity
  and cleanse me from my sin.
For I know my transgressions,
  and my sin is always before me.
Against you, you only, have I sinned
  and done what is evil in your
    sight."
Psalm 51:1-4

A promise to hang on to

• "If we confess our sins, [God] is faithful and just and will forgive us our sins and purify us from all unrighteousness." *1 John 1:9*

What to do when you're at your wits' end

Talk to yourself

The first sign of madness is *not* talking to yourself!

The psalmist often spoke to himself about his spiritual state: "My soul is downcast within me; therefore I will remember you [God]." *Psalm 42:6*

Honesty is the best policy

Nobody rejoiced in God more than the psalmist. But he also was honest enough to give voice to the times when he was feeling very low.

"Deep calls to deep
in the roar of your waterfalls;
all your waves and breakers
have swept over me."
Psalm 42:7

It's as if the psalmist is saying, "If you feel low, tell God about it, and admit it to yourself."

Questions and answers

Here are two questions the psalmist asked himself, and the answers he came up with, in Psalm 42.

- "Why are you downcast, O my soul? ... Put your hope in God."
- "Why so disturbed within me? ... I will yet praise him, my Savior and my God."

Turn to prayer

When we are down, we can turn to prayer, even though it may be the last thing we feel like doing.

Some reminders about prayer from the Psalms

- God loves to hear our prayers.
"God has surely listened
   and heard my voice in prayer.
Praise be to God,
   who has not rejected my prayer
   or withheld his love from me!"
Psalm 66:19-20

- Praise God for his love to you.
"Praise be to the LORD,
   for he showed his wonderful
   love to me."
Psalm 31:21

- Praise God for his greatness.
"I will praise you, O LORD, among
   the nations;
   I will sing of you among the
   peoples.
For great is your love, reaching to
   the heavens;
   your faithfulness reaches to the
   skies."
Psalm 57:9-10

- Tell God how great he is!
"As for God, his way is perfect;
   the word of the LORD is flawless.
He is a shield
   for all who take refuge in him.
For who is God besides the LORD?
   And who is the Rock except our
   God?"
Psalm 18:30-31

A promise to hang on to

"I guide you in the way of wisdom
and lead you along straight paths."
Proverbs 4:11

Time to make up your mind

Introduction

How do we decide on whether things are right or wrong, when there is nothing about them in the Ten Commandments? Where there is no one verse in the Bible to refer to, we have to try and see what the Bible's general teaching on the subject is. We should also find out whether Jesus gave any teaching on the subject.

Should I drink alcohol?

Christians vary in their answer to this question. Some say, "I never touch a drop." They have a very strong conviction that they should never drink a drop of alcohol, and even have unfermented grape juice, in place of wine, when they take part in the Lord's Supper.

Others ask, "What's wrong with a glass of wine with a meal, or having a drink at a party?"

Looking for the answer

• **Don't get drunk**
This is clearly taught in the Bible: "Do not get drunk on wine." *Ephesians 5:18*

• **Wine is a gift from God**
"[God] makes grass grow for the cattle,
  and plants for man to cultivate –
  bringing forth food from the earth:
wine that gladdens the heart of man,
  oil to make his face shine,
  and bread that sustains his heart."
Psalm 104:14-15

• **Wine as a medicine**
Paul tells his young friend, Timothy, who seems to have had a weak constitution: "Stop drinking only water, and use a little wine because of your stomach and your frequent illnesses." *1 Timothy 5:23*

Reaching different conclusions

In matters in which a vital principle of the Christian faith is not at stake, it is important that Christians do not expend a lot of energy on arguing with other Christians who hold different opinions to them.

Paul tried to prevent Christians from arguing with each other in this way:

"One man considers one day more sacred than another; another man considers every day alike. Each one should be fully convinced in his own mind. He who regards one day as special, does so to the Lord. He who eats meat, eats to the Lord, for he gives thanks to God; and he who abstains, does so to the Lord and gives thanks to God. For none of us lives to himself alone and none of us dies to himself alone. If we live, we live to the Lord; and if we die, we die to the Lord. So, whether we live or die, we belong to the Lord."
Romans 14:5-8

Should I gamble?

Bible principle to bear in mind: hard work is commended.

"If a man will not work, he shall not eat." *2 Thessalonians 3:10*

Is it okay to live together before marriage?

Bible principle to bear in mind: sexual immorality is decried.

Fornication is used figuratively to represent spiritual unfaithfulness to God:

"The body is not meant for sexual immorality, but for the Lord, and the Lord for the body. ... Flee from sexual immorality. All other sins a man commits are outside his body, but he who sins sexually sins against his own body."
1 Corinthians 6:13b, 18

Should I watch adult movies and videos?

Bible principle to bear in mind: our minds should be fed with uplifting thoughts and attitudes.

"Finally brothers, whatever is true, whatever is noble, whatever is right, whatever is pure, whatever is lovely, whatever is admirable – if anything is excellent or praiseworthy – think about such things." *Philippians 4:8*

"... I tell you that anyone who looks lustfully at a woman has already committed adultery with her in his heart." *Matthew 5:28*

Should I marry a non-Christian?

Do not be unequally yoked

The key verse many Christians turn to, when they are concerned about a Christian marrying a non-Christian, is: "Do not be yoked together with unbelievers." The King James Version translates this as "Be not unequally yoked ..."
2 Corinthians 6:14

In this verse, Paul is saying that to be closely partnered with an unbeliever is like trying to plough a field with two incompatible animals – like having an ox and a donkey hitched up together!

This verse says nothing about marriage. It could be applied to a close business partnership between a Christian and a non-Christian. But it is often cited as the reason Christians should not marry non-Christians.

The verses in 2 Corinthians 6:14-16 ask two other questions:
- What do righteousness and wickedness have in common?
- What harmony is there between Christ and Belial (another word for Satan)?

Remember *who* God is

During times when we feel that we don't want to hear what God says, what should we do? How should we react if we do not want to seek out God's guidance on some very personal matter?

We must remember that God wants the very best for us. And this comes from following his guidance.

Three Hebrew words

The way God guides us is seen in three Hebrew words:

• Nahag

This word means "to conduct along a path." God led the people of Israel out of their slavery in Egypt in this way.

"By day the LORD went ahead of them in a pillar of cloud to guide them on their way and by night in a pillar of fire to give them light, so that they could travel by day or night." *Exodus 13:21*

• Darak

This word means "to walk, to travel." The psalmist prayed that God would guide him in ways that would please God.

"Show me your ways, O LORD, teach me your paths; guide me in your truth and teach me,

for you are God my Savior, and my hope all day long." *Psalm 25:4-5*

• Nahal

This word means "to lead with care." It is the word used of a shepherd looking after his sheep. Isaiah the prophet comforted God's people when they thought that God had forsaken them.

"He tends his flock like a shepherd: He gathers the lambs in his arms and carries them close to his heart; he gently leads those that have young." *Isaiah 40:11*

Should I give my money to the poor?

Give a tenth of your income
In the Old Testament, God's people were told to give a tenth of their income for God's work, and for the poor. This instruction is not repeated in the New Testament.

So, should we give more or less than this?

Paul's advice
Paul outlines how we are to give money, and writes, "Each man should give what he has decided in his heart to give, not reluctantly or under compulsion, for God loves a cheerful giver." *2 Corinthians 9:7*
- Give it some thought.
- Do not give grudgingly.
- Give without being forced into doing it.
- Give cheerfully.

Giving everything away
This seems to have happened, on at least one occasion, in the early Church. "All the believers were together and had everything in common. Selling their possessions and goods, they gave to anyone as he had need." *Acts 2:44-45*

So, while there is no hint of this being compulsory, it certainly took place.

Jesus advises a rich young man

"As Jesus started on his way, a man ran up to him and fell on his knees before him. 'Good teacher,' he asked, 'what must I do to inherit eternal life?'

'Why do you call me good?' Jesus answered. 'No one is good – except God alone. You know the commandments: "Do not murder, do not commit adultery, do not steal, do not give false testimony, do not defraud, honor your father and mother."'

'Teacher,' he declared, 'all these I have kept since I was a boy.'

Jesus looked at him and loved him. 'One thing you lack,' he said. 'Go, sell everything you have and give to the poor, and you will have treasure in heaven. Then come, follow me.'"
Mark 10:17-21

Points to note
Jesus did not say this to every person he met. Clearly this rich man needed to hear this from Jesus so he could see that his money was more important to him than God's kingdom.

A sad ending
"At this the man's face fell. He went away sad, because he had great wealth. Jesus looked around and said to his disciples, 'How hard it is for the rich to enter the kingdom of God!'"
Mark 10:22-23

What to do when God's answer is "No"

God's answers

God answers all prayers. The answer may be "Yes," "No," or "Wait."

The apostle Paul was given the answer "No" to one of his prayers. He had some kind of illness, which he called his "thorn in the flesh." Paul prayed and prayed that God would heal him make him well.

"To keep me from becoming conceited because of these surpassingly great revelations, there was given me a thorn in my flesh, a messenger of Satan, to torment me. Three times I pleaded with the Lord to take it away from me. But he said to me, 'My grace is sufficient for you, for my power is made perfect in weakness.' Therefore I will boast all the more gladly about my weaknesses, so that Christ's power may rest on me." *2 Corinthians 12:7-9*

Bad times

When things are tough, or when things go wrong, it is even more important to know how one should behave as a Christian.

Continue to seek God's guidance

This needs faith. "And without faith it is impossible to please God, because anyone who comes to him must believe that he exists and that he rewards those who earnestly seek him." *Hebrews 11:6*

Be willing to do God's will

If we want to do something that we know is not God's will, it can be quite a severe test of our faith. If this happens, we need to choose to do God's will. Jesus said, "If anyone chooses to do God's will, he will find out whether my teaching comes from God or whether I speak of my own." *John 7:17*

Do not doubt God

Can we follow God's will for us without question?

"But when he asks, he must believe and not doubt, because he who doubts is like a wave of the sea, blown and tossed by the wind. That man should not think he will receive anything from the Lord; he is a double-minded man, unstable in all he does."
James 1:6-7

"You won't be heard, just because you pray a lot!"

There is a middle ground between persisting in prayer, and praying endlessly for the sake of it. Jesus once warned people about their long prayers.

"When you pray, do not keep on babbling like pagans, for they think they will be heard because of their many words. Do not be like them, for your Father knows what you need before you ask him."
Matthew 6:7-8

See also: *What to do when God seems distant*, page 38.

Five classic ways in which God guides

The classic guides

On pages 54-63, five classic ways of finding God's will are set out.
- God guides through inner conviction.
- God guides through prayer.
- God guides through circumstances.
- God guides through the Bible.
- God guides in unexpected ways.

Casting lots

In Bible times, one way people received God's guidance was by casting lots. Lots were two-sided discs. The way they landed when thrown was believed to denote God's will. In the Old Testament, land was divided up in this way. Lots were also used in the law courts. *See Joshua 18:10.*

> "Casting the lot settles disputes and keeps strong opponents apart." *Proverbs 18:18*

Matthias was chosen as a replacement apostle for Judas by casting lots.

> "Then they cast lots, and the lot fell to Matthias; so he was added to the eleven apostles."
> *Acts 1:26*

Urim and Thummin

The Jews had sacred lots called Urim and Thummin. These sacred lots were used by the high priest to find out God's will, especially in times of crisis.

> "Also put the Urim and the Thummin in the breastpiece, so they may be over Aaron's heart whenever he enters the presence of the LORD. Thus Aaron will always bear the means of making decisions for the Israelites over his heart before the LORD." *Exodus 28:30*

> "[Joshua] is to stand before Eleazar the priest, who will obtain decisions before him by inquiring of the Urim before the LORD." *Numbers 27:21*

Classic guide 1: God guides through inner conviction

The Holy Spirit as guide

The most important "inner" guide a Christian can have is the Holy Spirit. Jesus promised his first followers that "the Spirit of truth" would guide them "into all truth." *John 16:13*

- God's Spirit is in every Christian.
  "No one can say, 'Jesus is Lord,' except by the Holy Spirit."
  1 Corinthians 12:3

- God's Spirit makes God's will known to us.
  "But the Counselor, the Holy Spirit, whom the Father will send in my name, will teach you all things and will remind you of everything I have said to you." *John 14:26*

Conscience

Inner conviction should come from an educated conscience, not blind prejudice. Our thoughts, feelings, and conscience all need to be informed and molded by God's teaching from the Bible. Unless this happens, we may hold the strongest convictions in the world, but that in itself does not make us right.

- Obtaining an "educated" conscience
  "Oh, how I love your law!
    I meditate on it all day long.
  Your commands make me wiser
      than my enemies,
    for they are ever with me.
  I have more insight than all my
      teachers,
    for I meditate on your statutes."
  Psalm 119:97-99

Different types of conscience

- A weak conscience
Christians must look after those who have weak consciences, and prevent difficulties and temptations from being put in their way.
  "If anyone with a weak conscience sees you who have this knowledge eating in an idol's temple, won't he be emboldened to eat what has been sacrificed to idols? ... When you sin against your brothers in this way and wound their weak conscience, you sin against Christ." *1 Corinthians 8:10-12*

- A seared conscience
There are false teachers who deliberately try to turn Christians away from following Jesus, to evil paths.
  "The Spirit clearly says that in later times some will abandon the faith and follow deceiving spirits and things taught by demons.

Such teachings come through hypocritical liars, whose consciences have been seared as with a hot iron." *1 Timothy 4:1-2*

• A cleansed conscience
"How much more, then, will the blood of Christ, who through the eternal Spirit offered himself unblemished to God, cleanse our consciences from acts that lead to death, so that we may serve the living God!" *Hebrews 9:14*

• A clear conscience
"But do this with gentleness and respect, keeping a clear conscience, so that those who speak maliciously against your good behavior in Christ may be ashamed of their slander." *1 Peter 3:15-16*

• A good conscience
"Paul looked straight at the Sanhedrin and said, "My brothers, I have fulfilled my duty to God in all good conscience to this day."" *Acts 23:1*

A promise to hang on to
"The LORD will guide you always;
   he will satisfy your needs in a
     sun-scorched land
   and will strengthen your frame.
You will be like a well-watered
     garden,
   like a spring whose waters never
     fail."
Isaiah 58:11

Classic guide 2: God guides through prayer

Heart and prayer

We might infer from the Bible that it is not the length of our prayers, the position in which we pray, the words we use in our prayers, or whether our prayers are sung, said or unspoken that matter most. It is the state of our heart that counts. "In your hearts set apart Christ as Lord." *1 Peter 3:15*

Preparing hearts for prayer

• We need forgiven hearts
"He who conceals his sins does
    not prosper,
  but whoever confesses and
    renounces them finds mercy."
Proverbs 28:13

• We need humble hearts
"The sacrifices of God are a
    broken spirit;
  a broken and a contrite heart,
  O God, you will not despise."
Psalm 51:17

• We need obedient hearts
"Those who obey [Jesus']
commands live in him, and he in
them." *1 John 3:24*

• We need forgiving hearts
As he was being stoned to death,
"[Stephen] fell on his knees and
cried out, 'Lord, do not hold this
sin against them.'" *Acts 7:60*

Prayer requests

Jesus taught people to pray on their own, and to pray with others and for others.

"Again, I tell you that if two of you on earth agree about anything you ask for, it will be done for you by my Father in heaven. For where two or three come together in my name, there am I with them." *Matthew 18:19-20*

The power of group prayer in the Acts of the Apostles

• Before the Holy Spirit came
"They all joined together constantly in prayer, along with the women and Mary the mother of Jesus, and with his brothers." *Acts 1:14*

• "Set" forms of prayers
"They devoted themselves to the apostles' teaching and to the fellowship, to the breaking of bread and to prayer." *Acts 2:42*

• Prayer that shook the room
"After they prayed, the place where they were meeting was shaken." *Acts 4:31*

• A commissioning service
"So after they had fasted and prayed, they placed their hands on them and sent them off." *Acts 13:3*

Pray without ceasing

There is no place, or time, when you cannot pray.

Paul told his Christian friends at Thessalonica about one of the "secrets" of prayer – to pray all the time!

"Pray continually; give thanks in all circumstances." *1 Thessalonians 5:17-18*

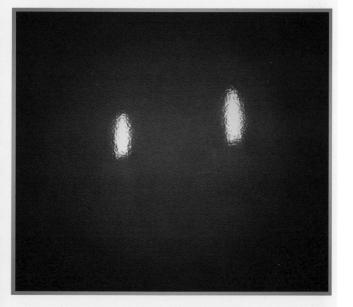

Classic guide 3: God guides through circumstances

Guidance and common sense

There's nothing wrong in being guided by common sense. God guided Paul through many seemingly ordinary situations.

How God guided Paul in "common sense" ways

• Bitten by a poisonous snake
"Paul gathered a pile of brushwood and, as he put it on the fire, a viper, driven out by the heat, fastened itself on his hand. When the islanders saw the snake hanging from his hand, they said to each other, "This man must be a murderer."" *Acts 28:3-4*

What did Paul do?
"Paul shook the snake off into the fire and suffered no ill-effects." *Acts 28:5*

• Fall from a window
"Paul spoke to the people and, because he intended to leave the next day, kept on talking until midnight. There were many lamps in the upstairs room where we were meeting. Seated in a window was a young man named Eutychus, who was sinking into a deep sleep as Paul talked on and on. When he was sound asleep, he fell to the ground from the third storey and was picked up dead." *Acts 20:7-9*

What did Paul do?
"Paul went down, threw himself on the young man and put his arms around him. 'Don't be alarmed,' he said. 'He's alive!' ... The people took the young man home alive and were greatly comforted." *Acts 20:10-12*

One of Paul's mottoes
"To the Jews I became like a Jew, to win the Jews. ...To those not having the law I became like one not having the law. ... I have become all things to all men so that by all possible means I might save some." *1 Corinthians 9:20-22*

One of Paul's strong beliefs
"We know that in all things God works for the good of those who love him, who have been called according to his purpose."
Romans 8:28

• The trial
Paul was on trial before two groups of people, the Pharisees and the Sadducees.

What did Paul do?
He managed to set his opponents against each other with his opening line of defence:
"Paul [facing the supreme Jewish court], knowing that some of them were Sadducees and the others Pharisees, called out in the Sanhedrin, 'My brothers, I am a Pharisee, the son of a Pharisee. I stand on trial because of my hope in the resurrection of the dead.' When he said this, a dispute broke out between the Pharisees and the Sadducees, and the assembly was divided. (The Sadducees say that there is no resurrection, and that there are neither angels nor spirits, but the Pharisees acknowledge them all.)
    There was a great uproar, and some of the teachers of the law who were Pharisees stood up and argued vigorously. 'We find nothing wrong with this man,' they said."
Acts 23:6-9

• A plot to kill Paul
"The next morning the Jews formed a conspiracy and bound themselves with an oath not to eat or drink until they had killed Paul. More than forty men were involved in this plot. They went to the chief priests and elders and said, 'We have taken a solemn oath not to eat anything until we have killed Paul. Now then, you and the Sanhedrin petition the commander to bring him before you on the pretext of wanting more accurate information about his case. We are ready to kill him before he gets here.'
    But when the son of Paul's sister heard of this plot, he went into the barracks and told Paul."
Acts 23:12-16

What did Paul do?
"Then Paul called one of the centurions and said, 'Take this young man to the commander; he has something to tell him.' So he took him to the commander."
Acts 23:17
    (This resulted in Paul being given an escort of "two hundred soldiers, seventy horsemen and two hundred spearmen."
Acts 23:23)

Classic guide 4: God guides through the Bible

The correct focus

Probably the greatest mistake we make about seeking God's will in our lives is to focus on ourselves instead of focusing on God.

• God exists. *Hebrews 11:6*
• God has a plan and purpose for our lives. *Jeremiah 1:4-5*
• God wants us to know about his plan. *Isaiah 30:21*

Right and wrong

One of the functions of the Bible is to tell us God's thoughts about right and wrong, and how we should think and behave.

• "The words of the LORD are flawless." *Psalm 12:6*
• "All Scripture is God-breathed and is useful for teaching, rebuking, correcting and training in righteousness, so that the man of God may be thoroughly equipped for every good work." *2 Timothy 3:16-17*

Commit your way to the Lord

One of the most helpful passages about guidance concerns committing ourselves to God. Notice the commands used in the following verses from Psalm 37: "Trust," "Delight," "Be still," "Wait patiently," and "Do not fret."

Psalm 37
"Trust in the LORD and do good,
   dwell in the land and enjoy safe pasture.
Delight yourself in the LORD
   and he will give you the desires of your heart.
Commit your way to the LORD;
   trust in him and he will do this:
He will make your righteousness shine like the dawn,
   the justice of your cause like the noonday sun.
Be still before the LORD and wait patiently for him;
   do not fret when men succeed in their ways,
   when they carry out their wicked schemes."
Psalm 37:3-7

Psalm 119

Just about all of the 176 verses of this psalm tell us something about God's word. The psalm uses eight different words to tell us the same basic thing.

• Law

"Blessed are they whose ways are blameless,

who walk according to the law of the LORD."

Psalm 119:1

"In the night I remember your name, O LORD,

and I will keep your law."

Psalm 119:55

• Statutes

"Blessed are they who keep his statutes

and seek him with all their heart."

Psalm 119:2

• Precepts

"You have laid down precepts that are to be fully obeyed."

Psalm 119:4

• Commands

"I seek you with all my heart;

do not let me stray from your commands."

Psalm 119:10

• Decrees

"You are good, and what you do is good;

teach me your decrees."

Psalm 119:68

• Word

"How can a young man keep his way pure?

By living according to your word."

Psalm 119:9

Classic guide 5: God guides in unexpected ways!

Balaam's donkey

Balaam's donkey must be about the most unusual way God used to guide anyone! A talking donkey, a disobedient prophet and an angel are the three participants in the story.

"When the donkey saw the angel of the LORD, she lay down under Balaam, and he was angry and beat her with his staff. Then the LORD opened the donkey's mouth, and she said to Balaam, 'What have I done to you to make you beat me these three times?'" *Numbers 22:27-28*

Balaam left this amazing incident, knowing that he now had to follow God's ways, with words from the angel ringing in his ear:

"Go ... but speak only what I tell you." *Numbers 22:35*

The Holy Spirit and the unexpected

In the New Testament God provided guidance through the Holy Spirit, but the 'means' by which this guidance came is not always mentioned. Much of the Holy Spirit's guidance was also most unexpected. It's almost if we are being taught to expect the unexpected.

Jesus

Jesus went into the desert to be tempted.

"Jesus, full of the Holy Spirit, returned from the Jordan and was led by the Spirit in the desert, where for forty days he was tempted by the Devil." *Luke 4:1-2*

Paul

Paul knew he would face serious dangers if he went to Jerusalem.

"And now, compelled by the Spirit, I am going to Jerusalem, not knowing what will happen to me there. I only know that in every city the Holy Spirit warns me that prison and hardships are facing me." *Acts 20:22-23*

All Christians

"Those who are led by the Spirit of God are children of God." *Romans 8:14*

The barriers of prejudice are smashed

Prejudice is hard to break. As a Jew, Peter was brought up to have little regard for non-Jews, Gentiles. No wonder it took an unexpected revelation to change Peter's thinking.

"[Peter] saw heaven opened and something like a large sheet being let down to earth by its four corners. It contained all kinds of four-footed animals, as well as reptiles of the earth and birds of the air. Then a voice told him, 'Get up, Peter. Kill and eat.'

'Surely not, Lord!" Peter replied. "I have never eaten anything impure or unclean.'

The voice spoke to him a second time, 'Do not call anything impure that God has made clean.'" *Acts 10:11-15*

This led Peter to do what he had previously thought was quite wrong. He went to the house of a Gentile, Cornelius the Roman centurion, and told his whole household about Jesus.

Can God "guide" me to do wrong?

David's temptation

David is tempted and encouraged to harm King Saul, who is trying to capture and kill him. But David refuses to kill Saul, even though he has opportunities to do it.

• **David's story**

"The men said, 'This is the day the LORD spoke of when he said to you, "I will give your enemy into your hands for you to deal with as you wish." ' Then David crept up unnoticed and cut off a corner of Saul's robe.

Afterwards, David was conscience-stricken for having cut off a corner of his robe. He said to his men, 'The LORD forbid that I should do such a thing to my master, the LORD's anointed, or lift my hand against him; for he is the anointed of the LORD.' "

1 Samuel 24:4-6

God's guidance is ...

• **For ever**

"For this God is our God for ever
    and ever;
   he will be our guide even to
    the end."
Psalm 48:14

• **On peaceful ways**

"[You will] guide our feet into the
    path of peace."
Luke 1:79

• **With his counsel**

"You guide me with your counsel,
    and afterwards you will take me
    into glory."
Psalm 73:24

• **On what is right**

"He guides the humble in what
    is right
   and teaches them his way."
Psalm 25:9